AWARENESS OF INDIRECTION

Francis Xavier Curzio

VANTAGE PRESS
New York / Washington / Atlanta
Los Angeles / Chicago

To Jean Darling,
my one and only,
a total devotion of a
wife to her husband's success

FIRST EDITION

All rights reserved, including the right of
reproduction in whole or in part in any form.

Copyright © 1987 by Francis X. Curzio

Published by Vantage Press, Inc.
516 West 34th Street, New York, New York 10001

Manufactured in the United States of America
ISBN: 0-533-07043-0

Library of Congress Catalog Card No.: 86-90092

CONTENTS

Preface v

Chapter I.	The Foundation	1
Chapter II.	Fundamental Analysis	7
Chapter III.	Diversity Categorized	20
Chapter IV.	Imperative Guidelines	29
Chapter V.	Avoidance of Disaster	34
Chapter VI.	The United States Government	41
Chapter VII.	Options	49
Chapter VIII.	Insider Trading—Insider Information	55
Chapter IX.	Interest Rates	58
Chapter X.	Conclusion	61

Epilogue 71

Glossary of Acronyms 73

PREFACE

In every profession, education is mandatory and experience a necessity. The stock market is no exception. It is a profession practiced by many, but mastered by few. This book is intended to provide basic, understandable guidelines about the ways of Wall Street for the inexperienced investor.

If you, as one of America's 40 million investors who annually contribute billions to the securities industry, wish to save and protect your investment dollar, you must learn to be aware. Assume personal responsibility for learning the fundamental analysis of stock evaluation. Always direct your attention to the quality of the stock, know the real value of one share, and beware of flashy advertising and biased journalism.

I am presenting some viable suggestions to help you become a shrewd investor rather than one of the thousands who, unfortunately, lose money because of lack of information or misrepresentation.

The viability of my investment premises may not be traditional, but they will help you perceive the real world of Wall Street's street-walkers, street-cleaners, and street-wise.

Apple sellers at 6th Avenue and 42nd Street. (Brown Brothers)

(This photo of apple sellers first appeared in *American History Illustrated* 14 [January 1980] and is used by permission.)

Chapter I

THE FOUNDATION

The Great Depression, why it happened and why it is unlikely to reoccur.

The Great Depression was preceded by other financial recessions. In 1921–22, for example, Americans experienced a brief period of economic distress, followed by the apparent seven fat years that were actually more bloat than fat. Many farmers, who had overextended themselves buying land with high crop profits during World War I, were in trouble when the war ended. When crop prices returned to lower levels, farmers were unable to sustain their profits. Others, who farmed marginal land, also suffered when the decline set in. Varying efforts were made to alleviate the agricultural decay of this era, including the Agricultural Marketing Act (AMA) of 1929, administered by the Federal Farm Board (FFB).
    Another reason for America's economic strife during the 1920s was the growing complexity of her industrial organization, primarily brought about by the advancement of the automobile, which expanded the worker's scope of employment to greater distances. Cities grew into huge, sprawling urban areas, creating serious economic distractions. Business cycles began evidencing a tendency

to higher peaks and deeper valleys. Americans found themselves facing financial discomfiture while becoming more dependent upon technology.

The late 1920s administration adhered to a policy of economic conservatism, determined to minimize government intervention. "Deflation must run its full course before prosperity could return" was the official attitude, instead of the "taking the bull by the horns" decisiveness, which was needed to curtail impending financial disaster.

September 3, 1929, marked the beginning, not of fortunes, but of failures. The paradoxical prosperity that had dominated the country began a process of rapid deterioration, triggering a general retrenchment. Stock prices soared upward; however, none but the shrewd perceived danger. Buyers, intoxicated with the optimistic thinking that they were marked for a speculative fortune, bought frantically with as little as a 10 percent down payment. Dow Jones averages reached their peak.

THE HOUSE COLLAPSES

On October 23, 1929, the stock market was at its all-time high, a high that would not be seen again until 1955, twenty-six years later. During the week of October 24 to October 29, stocks collapsed completely. An epitomized symbol of this disaster appeared on a 1933 *Vanity Fair* cover: "Cut outs" from newspaper stock tables revealed American Power and Light crashing from 156 to an emaciated 4½.

On October 24, 1929, before the first hour of trading was over, stock prices were tumbling. Thirteen million shares were sold, many by brokers protecting themselves when the customer's margin of ownership was gone. The stock ticker ran hours late as blocks of stock were dumped on the market. The stock exchanges were chaotic; pandemonium swept the nation. Five days later came catastrophe.

On October 29, 1929 (Black Tuesday), 16,500,000 shares were unloaded, a record that would not be broken until thirty years later. The entire financial world staggered in disbelief as blue chips, including American Telephone and Telegraph, General Electric, and General Motors, lost from 100 to 200 points in a five-day span. The ensuing panic created economic failures that shattered world economies for a decade.

At first the largest investors were the hardest hit, but it wasn't long before thousands of smaller ones watched what little assets they had dissolve and disappear. Between the high of October 23 and the low of November 12, 1929, the price of fifty leading stocks was cut in half. No one quite knew what had happened: One day the sun just didn't rise, creating ten years of financial darkness.

Over $45 billion in capital had vanished, a figure representing half the gross national product. In five days the Dow Jones average had dropped approximately 50 percent, over 180 points. From a high of 380 in 1929, it dropped to a mere forty in 1932. This failure was initiated by various factors: greed, excessive speculation, unrealistic government policies, and control of wealth by an elitist minority.

The secretary of the treasury, for example, felt that the financial situation was not sufficiently menacing to warrant pessimism and anticipated that by New Year's Day, 1930, improvement would be evident to the nation. However, this was incorrect; during the winter of 1930–31, unemployment was over four million. By March 31, 1931, unemployment skyrocketed to eight million. One out of three Americans was looking for work.

Meanwhile, banks were closing at an alarming rate; 1,300 had failed, suspending operations. Later, the number was a mind-boggling 5,000. The summer of 1931 also saw a European economic situation deteriorate severely. The Kreditanstalt, Austria's most influential bank, was in serious difficulty. News of this soon spread fear throughout Europe. German and British institutions were feeling the heat of a financial furnace set ablaze by the depression. England abandoned the gold standard, a move that dropped the prices of foreign investments on the New York Stock Exchange. This affected U.S. banks, creating a new wave of hoarding.

In the spring of 1933, long lines, mostly of men, stood cold and dejected, waiting hours for a handout of free bread. Millionaires peddled apples; others wore signs on their backs saying, I must have work, or I'll starve. Business and industry came to a halt. Thirteen million wage earners were unemployed; five million families became dependent on charity. Factories operated part-time and many businesses closed. Farmers were subjected to the largest drought in history. The tragedy of the Joad family, poignantly told by John Steinbeck in his American classic, *The Grapes of Wrath*, was also the story of thousands of other farm families. The plight of the agricultural sector and subsequent lack of crops contributed greatly to the extent of the depression.

Much needed to be done to stem the panic and hysteria that had gripped our nation. America was collapsing under the financial and physical strain. The nation's leaders belatedly perceived the necessity to introduce governmental measures of protection against present and future financial collapse.

THE NEW DEAL—REBUILDING THE FOUNDATION

During March 9 through June 16, 1933, a period known as the "Hundred Days," various crucial bills were passed through Congress. On March 9, the Emergency Banking Relief Act (EBRA) was passed. It called in all the gold and provided for reopening of banks. Within a few days, banks began to operate again. By March 16, three-quarters of the Federal Reserve Banks were operating.

Even the New York Stock Exchange was reestablishing itself, beginning to show signs of life. The Dow Jones Industrial Average traded at sixty, up 50 percent from its 1932 low of forty, a year past.

Several measures to alleviate the stress felt by farmers were also passed by Congress. The Agricultural Adjustment Administration (AAA) was designed to control farm production. The Farm Credit Administration (FCA) loaned money to farmers.

Another bill of great significance was the Federal Deposit Insurance Corporation (FDIC). This provided a new form of protection for depositors, initially insuring each for $10,000; today each depositor is insured for up to $100,000. The National Labor Relations Act (NLRA) gave workers the right to organize into unions and negotiate with company management. This initiated an unprecedented opportunity for the average citizen to wield more control over the nation's distribution of wealth and powers.

In 1933 Congress also created the Tennessee Valley Authority (TVA), which dramatically upgraded living conditions in the eight-state area drained by the Tennessee River.

The Securities Exchange Commission (SEC), established in 1933, became the investor's guardian by curbing dishonesty and potential manipulation of stock market operations.

The programs that evidenced the most powerful impact, however, were the Public Works programs. In 1933 the Public Works Administration (PWA) supervised the erection of public buildings and various construction projects. The Civilian Conservation Corps (CCC) enlisted young men into conservation camps, employing them in such areas as flood control, road building, and foresting. Work was provided for 250,000 men between the ages of eighteen to twenty-five, wages were thirty dollars per month, and ultimately a total of two million participated.

A similar plan, the Works Project Administration (WPA), begun in 1935, also employed millions, accomplishing many gainful ventures.

Another major bill achieving great impact in alleviating the suffering created by the depression was the Social Security Act (SSA). Passed by Congress in 1935, it set up two kinds of social insurance: one provided for old-age and disability insurance; the other provided unemployment insurance. Late 1936, the Dow Jones Averages traded at 180, up 350 percent from its 1932 low of forty points. It would take another nineteen years for the averages to double (a 100 percent gain) and eventually trade above the October 23, 1929, high of 380 points.

In 1939, the Federal Security Agency (FSA) was established to supervise social security and welfare activities. In 1953 this agency became our present Department of Health, Education, and Welfare.

These varied congressional acts contributed momentously to the stabilization of our shattered economy and to the restoration of productive order. American leadership, through congressional measures, had thus provided a foundation of financial security for all citizens. In the following chapters, specific information will be presented to you, the investor, to enable you to take advantage of this foundation and progress to personal gain.

Chapter II

FUNDAMENTAL ANALYSIS

Simple accounting principals that must be known before investing in a situation.

Every day, thousands of individuals waste money by paying excessive amounts for stocks worth just a smidgen of their real value. When buying a stock, you are buying a share; consequently you must know the real value of one (1) share of stock, not the psychological value. The Securities and Exchange Commission (SEC) requires all public companies to furnish their shareholders with an annual report, to file a "10K" (expanded annual report) and a "10Q" (quarterly report) with the commission. The SEC will send you the "10K" and "10Q" of any company for a small fee. Always read these reports, studying carefully the figures presented on the balance sheet and on the income statement. These figures tell the real story. A company will always laud optimistic views regarding their prospects; brokers and friends will often tout their favorite stocks. Protect yourself by requesting the latest "10K" and "10Q." Incidentally, most companies will furnish a complimentary copy of their reports upon written request.

Investor Information References:

Disclosure Inc.: 5161 River Road, Bethesda, MD 20816. Tele: 800-638-8241. Will forward requests for companies 10K's ($25, per 10K) and 10Q's ($5, per 10Q). First class mail or same-day service.

Federal Document Retrieval: 504 C Street, N.E., Washington, DC 20002. Also provides investor retrieval services. Tele: 202-628-2229.

U.S. Securities Exchange Commission: 450 Fifth Street N.W., Washington, D.C. 20549. Tele: 202-655-4000.

THE BALANCE SHEET

Remember, you are purchasing a stock based on its one (1) share evaluation. If one share is worth $1.00, 100 shares are worth $100.00, 1,000 shares, $1,000.00. The following are comparative balance sheets of one model company, the Baby Corporation:

Assets:	December 31:1986	1985
Current Assets:		
Cash	$ 50,000,000	$ 45,000,000
Accounts receivables	200,000,000	175,000,000
Inventories	420,000,000	370,000,000
Prepaid expenses	30,000,000	10,000,000
Total current Assets:	$ 700,000,000	$ 600,000,000
Other Assets:		
Land and buildings	$ 150,000,000	$ 120,000,000
Machinery and equipment	80,000,000	70,000,000
Furniture and fixtures	50,000,000	60,000,000
Miscellaneous	20,000,000	30,000,000
Total other Assets:	$ 300,000,000	$ 280,000,000
Total Assets:	$1,000,000,000	$ 880,000,000

Liabilities and Stockholders Equity:

Current Liabilities:

Notes payable	$ 77,000,000	$ 97,000,000
Accounts payable	140,000,000	130,000,000
Income taxes payable	20,000,000	25,000,000
Other	113,000,000	140,000,000
Total current liabilities:	$ 350,000,000	$392,000,000
Long Term Debt:	$ 150,000,000	$110,000,000
Total liabilities:	$ 500,000,000	$502,000,000

Stockholders Equity:
Common stock:

100,000,000 shares authorized	$ 200,000,000	$200,000,000
50,000,000 outstanding		
Retained earnings	300,000,000	178,000,000
Total Stockholders Equity:	$ 500,000,000	$378,000,000
Total liabilities and Stockholders Equity:	$1,000,000,000	$880,000,000

Most corporation balance sheets show results of two years, although government regulations are trending toward a five-year disclosure. For simplification, our example, the Baby Corporation, shows a two-year comparative balance sheet.

Studying the balance sheet of a corporation should be your first priority because it most accurately reflects the financial health of the company. It provides you with the imperative information of the exact collateral behind each share of stock.

BALANCE SHEET TERMS

Understanding the following terms should facilitate basic analysis of stock worth:

Assets: Anything of value to the corporation.
Current Assets: Assets that can easily be converted into cash.
Liability: A debt; any amount owed.
Current Liabilities: A debt due within one year.
Long Term Debt: A debt (liability) due after one year (example: mortgages).
Stockholder's Equity and Net Worth: Assets less liabilities (actual worth of the company).
Retained Earnings: Accumulation of company's earnings since origination of company, less dividends paid out to shareholders. (Retained earnings are included in stockholder's equity).
Working Capital: Current assets less current liabilities (amount of money a company has left after paying current debts).
Current Ratio: The ratio by which current assets exceed current liabilities. (This ratio is determined by dividing the current liabilities into the current assets).

Since the current ratio explicitly reflects the financial health of a company, note this further explanation. Say, for example, as with the Baby Corporation, a company has twice as many current assets as current liabilities:

$$\frac{\text{Current assets} \quad \$700{,}000{,}000}{\text{Current liabilities} \quad \$350{,}000{,}000} = 2 \text{ or } 2.0{:}1 \text{ Current ratio.}$$

Then Baby is in good financial health, as a small company with assets less than $100 million should have a current ratio of 2.0:1 or better; however, a large company's current ratio should be 1.5:1 or better. To summarize, it's not necessary to be an accounting major to deal successfully with stocks; it's sufficient that you know the difference between an asset and a liability and that you are cognizant that this difference equates the stock-

holder's equity, or a company's net worth.
To exemplify this last point:

Current assets:	$700,000,000	Total assets:	$1,000,000,000
Less: current liabilities:	(350,000,000)	Total liabilities:	
Working capital:	$350,000,000	Stockholders equity:	(500,000,000) $ 500,000,000

Other aids to perceptive investing are publications such as *Standard & Poor's Stock Guide*, referred to as "The Bible of the Industry." This guide states the current assets and liabilities of over 5,000 companies and provides reliable information. The *Value Line Survey* is also useful. It provides more extensive information about financial histories of approximately 1,900 companies.

Sample Data

Company Name	Current Assets	Current Liabilities	Current Ratio
Bishop Graphics	$ 5 Million	$ 2 Million	2.5:1
Black Industries	$ 6 "	$ 1 "	6.1:1
Long Island Lighting	$ 587 "	$ 391 "	1.5:1
Mor-Flo Industries	$ 80 "	$ 40 "	2.0:1
Santa Fe So. Pac.	$ 2,300 "	$ 1,460 "	1.6:1
Skyline Corp.	$ 110 "	$ 20 "	5.5:1
United Oil & Gas	$ 20 "	$ 60 "	0.3:1

An investor interpreting this given data should note: Bishop Graphics has 2.5 times more current assets; Black Industries has six times more assets; Long Island Lighting has 1.5 times more assets; Santa Fe has 1.6 times more assets; Mor-Flo has two times more assets; Skyline Corporation has 5.5 times more assets; however, United Canso Oil & Gas has current liabilities that exceed its current assets by three times.

The investor's conclusion should be that the first six companies listed deserve further investigation, but United Canso's debt cancels any reasons for consideration. The company that lacks excess cash (liquidity) also lacks strength to weather economic downturns and is a poor investment choice. United Canso in June 1981 traded at $23 a share. Two years later the stock traded at less than $1 a share; the interest on debt resulted in millions of dollars of losses and no near term solution to pay off its debt due to the oil and gas industry's economic downturn.

LONG TERM DEBT

A company's long-term debt (loans or debt due after 1 year) should not exceed its current assets. For example, the Baby Corporation 1986 balance sheet shows current assets of $700 million vs. a long-term debt of $150 million, reflecting a continued healthy financial position.

Analyzing Data

Company Name	Long Term Debt	Current Assets
Bishop Graphics	$ 1 Million	$ 5 Million
Black Industries	$ 1 "	$ 6 "
Long Island Lighting	$ 2 Billion	$587 "
Mor-Flo Industries	$30 Million	$ 98 "
Santa Fe Southern Pac.	$ 2 Billion	$ 2 Billion
Skyline Corp.	$ 1 Million	$110 Million

Evaluating this data, the investor should take Long

Island Lighting (LIL) off his list, regardless of its blue chip enticement. Interest on $2 billion at 10 percent annually is $200 million. Based on these figures, in two and a half years from the time of this financial disclosure, LIL would have used all its assets to pay interest.

In 1984, LIL actually was in serious financial trouble because the current assets of $587 million vs. the current liabilities of $391 million left an excess of only $196 million working capital. Subsequently, LIL failed to make interest and debt payments, bringing the company to a tenuous hold on solvency, as its stock plunged from $27 to a devastating $3 a share. Long-term followers of the market may remember a similar occurrence of a blue chip converting into a potato chip, the 1972 fiasco of Penn Central Stock sinking from $86 to less than $1 a share.

The lesson to be learned from these examples is that an informed investor will shrewdly avoid being overconfident about a stock just because it is blue chip; he will check reliable sources of information and will purchase stock on the basis of evaluating a company's current assets, current liabilities, and total long-term debt.

However, if you can afford to indulge in a speculative situation (which is discussed further in chapter 3 under "Diversity Categorized"), LIL at $3 a share presented itself as worth a several-hundred dollar speculative buy because the stock price reflected the situation, and LIL could not shut down its generators.

BOOK VALUE

Book value, an accounting term, is determined by adding all assets of a company, then deducting all liabilities.

This figure, which is noted on the balance sheet as stockholder's equity, is then divided by the number of common shares outstanding, and the result is book value per common share.

To exemplify, again using the 1986 balance sheet for the Baby Corporation:

Stockholders equity	=	$500 Million
Shares outstanding	=	50 Million
$500 million ÷ $50 million	=	$10 a share

This book value of $10 a share, however, may have little relationship to the market value of a share. For example, a company has assets exceeding the value that is listed on the balance sheet, such as Santa Fe Southern Pacific (SFX). Assume that SFX has a book value of $30 a share; the land it acquired in the 1800s is recorded on its books at the original cost, but that same land today is probably worth many times the original value. (Accounting standards prohibit a write-up of assets due to appreciation.) Consequently, a justifiable market value for each share may be many times its book value. Generally, the book value per share should not exceed twice the market value. Buying a stock at less than its book value is a plus because we know book value is comprised of assets.

Sample Analysis of Book Value and Market Price

Company Name	Book Value			Market Price	Recommend
		Per	Share		BUY
Bishop Graphics	$ 3.00	"	"	$ 4.00	"
Black Industries	$ 5.75	"	"	$ 4.50	"
Mor-Flo Industries	$10.00	"	"	$12.00	"
Santa Fe Southern Pacific	$30.00	"	"	$15.00	"
Skyline Corp.	$11.00	"	"	$12.50	"

Based on the above data, the prudent investor may prefer Black Industries on the market at less than book value per share. Black Industries traded over twice its book value in late 1985, up over 200 percent from its 1984 market price, and Santa Fe traded at $35 a share, up over 100 percent from its market price in 1983. Investors had the opportunity to purchase both stocks at substantial discounts to book value.

EMPHASIZE PER SHARE VALUE

If, for example, the Baby Corporation's stockholder's equity was $500 million (as in our previous example), and its shares outstanding were 500 million rather than 50 million, then the book value would be $1 a share.

$$\frac{\text{Stockholder's Equity}}{\text{Shares Outstanding}} \quad \frac{500 \text{ million}}{500 \text{ million shares}} = \$1 \text{ per share (book value)}$$

We can readily see that the stock's book value is $1 a share. If the stock is trading at $10 a share or more, you had better find a hidden asset on the company's balance sheet.

The speculative investor should also be cautious about the penny stock fad which is often a sucker play for the uninformed: these are stocks which have book values less than one-tenth of one cent a share. Yet investors think they are going to strike it rich buying the stock at a penny a share. One penny in this case is 1,000 percent over book value. No company is worth in excess of two times its book value—unless it holds vast quantities of undervalued real estate or huge reserves of oil, the value of which is not reflected in its assets on its balance sheet. If so, the market price of the stock usually reflects such value.

In summary, the main points to ask yourself when assessing a company's balance sheet are these:

1. What is the book value or stockholder's equity per share?

2. How does this book value compare to actual market price per share?
3. What is the current ratio?
4. What is the company's long-term debt position?

THE INCOME STATEMENT

The price—earnings (P/E) ratio is the price of a share of stock divided by earnings per share for a twelve-month period. This popular way of comparing stocks selling at various price levels is a good instrument for an investor if he studies a company's income statement carefully, concentrating on the income per share rather than total income.

Income Statement Ended December 31, 1986

	Company A	Company B
Operating revenues:	$100,000,000	$100,000,000
Expenses: Cost of goods sold	$50,000,000	$50,000,000
Selling and administrative	$20,000,000	$20,000,000
Depreciation	$10,000,000	$10,000,000
Income from operations:	$20,000,000	$20,000,000
Less Income taxes:	$10,000,000	$10,000,000
Net income:	$10,000,000	$10,000,000
Shares outstanding:	1 Million	10 Million

Both companies reported the same profits, but Company B has ten times or 1,000 percent more shares outstanding than Company A.

Assuming each company's financial position is sound, your next criteria for purchasing a stock is its earnings per share. Company A earned $10 million and has one million shares outstanding. Company B earned $10 million but has ten million shares outstanding. We now must differentiate earnings per share by dividing the net profit by the shares outstanding.

Company A: Net Profit: $10 Million = $10 per share
Shares Outstanding: 1 Million Shares
Company B: Net Profit: $10 Million
Shares Outstanding: 10 Million shares = $1 per share

Practically all annual reports and quarterly reports state earnings per share (EPS).

As we can easily compare, Company A should command approximately ten times the market price of Company B, for the growth on your buying one share of stock in Company A is ten times that of Company B. Security analysts use the price earnings ratio (P/E ratio) when comparing company earnings. It is a relationship between a stock's market price and its earnings per share, arrived at by dividing a company's earnings per share into the market price of the stock. Let's assume Company A sells for $50 per share and Company B is selling at $10 per share:

Company A:
Market Price: $50 per share = 5 times earnings (P/E ratio
Earnings per share: $10 per share of 5)

Company B:
Market Price: $10 per share = 10 times earnings (P/E ratio
Earnings per share: $1 per share of 10)

Company A has a P/E ratio of five. Company B has a P/E ratio of ten. It would require five years of earnings to equal your purchase price or investment in Company A if earnings remained the same. It would require ten years of earnings to equal your purchase price in Company

B. Therefore, even though Company B stock sells at $10 per share, Company A is the better buy at $50 per share.

Barron's, U.S.A. Today, and other local newspapers list the P/E ratios of listed stocks on the New York Stock Exchange and the American Stock Exchange.

Remember, emphasize per share data: book value per share, stockholder's equity or net worth per share, and earnings per share. Price–earnings ratio (P/E Ratio) is used when comparing earnings vs. market price in relation to other companies.

The lower the price–earnings ratio, usually the less downside risk involved. The vital issue is not today's earnings per share, but rather tomorrow's earnings per share. A financially strong company should maintain its status and outperform its competitors.

In an expanding economy, a financially strong company probably will increase its earnings faster than a weak company. In a recession, a strong company not only will survive, it probably will be able to sell its product at lower prices than a weaker company that must be concerned with paying its debts and surviving. Also, companies with debt pay part of their profits to the banks in the form of interest. Little or no debt companies pay their profits to stockholders or reinvest their profits back into the company, thereby increasing the company book value and future earnings potential.

CONCLUSION

When purchasing a stock it is imperative you know:

1. The company's current financial position: current ratio.
2. The company's long-term debt position: loans & interest expense.
3. The book value per share: the company's real value per share.

Price–earnings (P/E) ratio vs. other P/E ratios of stocks in related industries is also important. Companies with good management and strong financial positions will earn profits and will indeed get market recognition.

You must be in a position to successfully distinguish weak stocks from quality stocks, thereby avoiding the 18,000 overvalued stocks vs. the 2,000 quality issues that are trading on the various exchanges and the Over-The-Counter (OTC) market. It is important to reread and understand this chapter: comprehending these financial facts will facilitate your potential for success. As an informed investor, you will be in a position to distinguish quality from quantity.

Chapter III

DIVERSITY CATEGORIZED

Conservative and speculative investments classified into six simple categories.

There are two classes of investments, conservative and speculative. Conservative investments usually entail less risk than speculative investments. All investments entail risk, but the risk can be spread by diversifying into more than one situation.

Conservative Situations:
Utility Stocks   Preferred Stocks
Bonds   Convertible Preferred Stocks
Convertible Bonds   Common Stocks
CATS—Certificates of Accrual on Treasury Securities

Speculative Situations: Any venture which entails above average risk, given the potential or chance of making large profits. Speculative situations are usually confined to purchases of small company stocks, opened options and commodity contracts purchased on margin.

Conservative and speculative situations are categorized as follows:

Asset Plays
Growth Stocks
High-Tech Situations

Income Situations
Special Situations
Turnaround Situations

There are two classes of investments and six different categories.

DEFINITION OF CATEGORIES

ASSET PLAYS: A company whose assets are not reflected in the price of the stock. Examples: Real estate holdings, patents, copywrites, natural resource leaseholdings, in-ground reserves of oil, gas, precious metals, et cetera (most takeover candidates are in this category). Moderate risk–high reward.

Canada Southern Petroleum Ltd. (CSW.P)   Exxon Corp. (XON)
Burke-Parsons-Bowlby (BPAB)   Santa Fe Southern Pacific (SFX)

GROWTH STOCKS: A company that has a consistent record of sales and per share earnings growth. Moderate risk–moderate reward.

American Home Products (AHP)   McDonald's Corp. (MCD)
International Business Machines (IBM)   Syntex Corp. (SYN)

HIGH-TECH SITUATIONS: A company that shows prospects of earnings growth due to its technological expertise in its respective field. Very risky–high reward.

Boeing Co. (BA)   Rockwell International (ROK)
Bishop Graphics (BGPH)   Mor-Flo Ind. (MORF)

INCOME SITUATIONS: Suitable for Individual Retirement Accounts (IRA). Utility, preferred stocks and bonds. For IRA's, they represent compounding of tax-free dividends and interest. (The least speculative and most conservative category).

Utility Stocks
Bonds
Preferred Stocks
CATS—Certificates of Accrual on Treasury Securities

SPECIAL SITUATIONS: A company whose assets and stock price may increase significantly as a result of a favorable litigation settlement, takeover, extraordinary profit, large contract or a technological breakthrough. Usually speculative but near term explosive price appreciation possible.

Black Industries (BLAK)
Canada Southern Petroleum (CSW.P)
Groff Industries, Inc. (GROF)

TURN-AROUND SITUATIONS: A company that may report significant per share earnings versus a prior year's loss, or poor earnings performance. Moderately speculative. Usually the current stock price is low, reflecting the company's past poor performance.

American Ship Building (ABG)
Bethlehem Steel PFD. (BS.PR)
Diamond Shamrock (DIA)
Ford Motor(F)
Lone Star Ind. PFD. (LCE.PR)
Skyline Corp. (SKY)

BONDS: GENERAL INFORMATION

Bonds: a bond is a borrowing. No matter who the issuer may be—corporation, federal government or agency, state or local municipality—a bond is a debt obligation. A bond is a borrowing—by the debt issuer. Like any debt, the bond is a promise to repay a loan at a specified time, with interest paid at set dates during its life. A corporation or a government agency offers a bond issue in the open market to raise money.

Mortgage bonds and debentures: Except for municipal bonds, there are two types of debt obligations: (1) collateralized—backed by a lien or call on certain stipulated assets; (2) those which are not collateralized. The term *mortgage bonds* refers to collateralized obligations. Unsecured debt obligations are called *debentures*. Generally, debt obligations which are collateralized are superior in quality to those which are not.

Par value: In looking at bond prices, you should keep in mind that par is the dollar value of the bond, upon which interest is figured. Par value is $1,000; price quotes are on that basis. Thus a bond priced at 100 really means $1,000, while one quoted at ninety-nine really means $990. Similarly a price 103 would mean $1,030. Each point advance or decline in a bond equals $10.

Fluctuation: The prices of fixed income obligations fluctuate in response to changes in the current interest rate. If interest rates decline, bond prices will rise, and vice versa. The reason for this is that the income paid by bonds is fixed. For example, a bond paying $100 in interest and offered at $1,000, or par, would yield 10 percent. However, if the going rate of interest rises to 12 percent the price of the bond must decline accordingly to adjust the value of its $100 income to the going rate. Similarly, if the going interest rate declines, the price of the bond will go up. Bond prices must adjust to changes in the going interest rate, since their own income cannot change.

Fluctuation in corporate bonds will also be influenced by the assets and earnings of the corporation. *Standard & Poor's* bond rating system has AAA as the highest rating assigned indicating that capacity to pay interest and repay principal is extremely strong. D is the lowest rating indicating that payment of interest and/or repayment of principal is in arrears. Your broker or the

company will provide you with the specific bond rating.
Investors should always have on hand a *Standard & Poor's (S&P) Bond and Stock Guide.*

Investors information references:

Standard & Poor's Corporation
25 Broadway,
New York, New York 10004
Tele: (212) 208-8769

Bond Guide (1 monthly issue)	$12.00
approximately 225 pages Annually: (12 monthly issues)	$138.00
Stock Guide (1 monthly issue)	$9.00
approximately 250 pages Annually: (12 monthly issues)	$78.00

Maturity dates and coupon rate: All bonds have a maturity date when the debt is to be repaid. It may be a specific date or it may be set in a serial form with certain amounts of the total issue falling due at different times. The interest paid by a bond (often called the coupon rate) is a fixed amount to be paid on specified dates, usually quarterly or semiannually.

Sinking fund: Many bonds will have sinking funds. This means that after some time a stipulated amount of the bond issue (usually very small) will be retired (bought back) each year. The purpose of a sinking fund is to reduce the issue substantially before the maturity date arrives. The issuer may call the issue or any part of it—that is, pay off the borrowing—at any time before maturity date. The price at which the bond is retired is usually greater than the par value (100) by an amount equal to about one year's interest.

The conversion feature: A convertible bond issued by a corporation may have a conversion feature which offers holders the right at their discretion to convert the bond into shares of the company's common stock. This gives the holders a chance to participate in the growth of the company through, in effect, a call on its common stock. This feature often reflects the fact that the issue cannot command the lower interest rates accorded higher quality issues; the conversion feature is thus a sweetener—part of an effort to obtain a lower interest rate.

A bond's unique quality: A bond will rank ahead of a preferred stock or common stock in its claim to assets if a company is liquidated. It also has first call on the available earnings (dividends to shareholders) ahead of preferred stock or common stock. In addition, the interest on a bond must be paid (remember, it's a debt obligation), and failure to do so could invite foreclosure.

Zero Coupon Bonds

Certificates of Accrual on Treasury Securities (CATS): CATS represent direct interests in U.S. Treasury notes or bonds. Zeros sell for a fraction of their face value of $1,000. Instead of paying semiannual interest, the interest is compounded over the life of the zero coupon bond. At maturity, you receive the full face value of $1,000. CATS are traded on the New York Bond Exchange (NYBE). The NYBE is listed in most major newspapers. CATS possess liquidity and can be purchased or sold at any time prior to maturity.

Even though you do not receive the interest until the note or bond matures, you are subject to pay taxes on the interest. The exception is when they are purchased for your Individual Retirement Account (IRA) or Keogh Retirement Plan.

Analyzing Data

	Maturity Date	Years to Maturity	Current Price	Price Range	Total Return
*CATS ZR	1988	4	$630	$580-$670	59%
" ZR	1991	7	420	300-460	144%
" ZR	1994	10	350	290-390	286%
" ZR	1995	11	310	270-360	323%
" ZR	1996	12	250	220-310	400%
" ZR	1997	13	220	210-270	476%
" ZR	1999	15	180	160-260	588%
" ZR	2001	17	140	130-180	714%

The total return is guaranteed and the notes and bonds offer the highest degree of safety and security.

Given today's high interest rates, consider CATS as a must. The Dow Jones would have to trade at 1,746 in 1988 to return the guaranteed principal of the CATS ZR 1988. In ten years the Dow Jones would have to trade at 3,143 to return the guaranteed principal of the CATS ZR 1994, and in 17 years the Dow Jones would have to trade at 7,859 to return the guaranteed principal of the CATS ZR 2001.

Some of the greatest growth stocks in Wall Street history have never recorded appreciation as presented here. In bull or bear markets, inflationary or deflationary cycles, recession or boom, CATS represent the ultimate safety coupled with guaranteed compounded return.

If interest rates drop, CATS will appreciate well before maturity. In time, given stable current interest rates CATS will appreciate accordingly. An example of this is the ZR CAT 1991 currently at $420, which will trade at $630 three years from now. You don't have to wait to

*Listed daily in the *Wall Street Journal* and weekly in *Barron's* under the heading "The New York Bond Exchange."

maturity to reap substantial gains.

Caution: If prevailing interest rates rise, the value of the CATS will decline more than conventional bonds. If CATS are held to maturity, short-term losses are simply paper losses.

YIELD

Dividend: When a company is making money it usually rewards its shareholders by paying them a portion of its profits (dividends). Dividend income paid to common stock holders may increase or decrease based on the company's profit.

When buying conservative stocks, always purchase a stock that not only pays a dividend, but increases its dividend (usually annually) as profits increase. This concept reflects the fact that the management of the company is stock market conscious.

Dividend-paying stocks usually perform better than nondividend-paying stocks. Always check to see if the earnings per share can support the current dividend per share. If the company is earning $1 a share and pays $.30 a share to its stockholders in dividends, there is room for future dividend increases. If the company is earning $1 a share and pays $.90 a share in dividends, not only is there no room for a dividend increase, but if earnings decline, the dividend may be cut or even omitted.

Cuts and omissions of dividends have resulted in the largest losses incurred by conservative investors. The institutional managers will sell (dump) stocks on the market for whatever price they can get when faced with adverse financial conditions regarding a stock they hold in their portfolio. The exception is, the profit potential should not be overlooked in a stock that fell 50% or more in price due to a dividend cut if the fundamentals reflect a continued sound financial position, and the book value per share is less than the current market price.

Interest: Interest income from a bond is usually a fixed amount. There are some bonds that pay interest based on the U.S. Treasury bill rates, or the interest rates which fluctuate; however, bond interest payments generally do not fluctuate.

Chapter IV

IMPERATIVE GUIDELINES

Realizing your gains while limiting your risks. The "Stop-Loss" strategy.

Chapter 1 briefly discussed the stock market crash, the great depression and subsequent government controls that virtually eliminate a recurrence of another Great Depression. Chapter 2 delineated financial fundamentals that must be known by you prior to making an investment decision. Chapter 3 delineated diversity. This chapter will emphasize our imperative guidelines:

1. Speculate with a small portion of your funds.
2. Invest in ten to fifteen situations (stocks and bonds)—diversity.
3. Do not buy on margin.
4. If any stock doubles in value, sell half.
5. Have patience.

   1. Speculate with a small portion of your funds. Invest a little to make a lot, and not a lot to make a little. Invest $1,000 to make a minimum of $2,000. Do not invest $10,000 to make $2,000. Invest $10,000 to make $20,000.
   2. Buy a minimum of ten speculative and conserva-

tive situations. Purchasing a highly speculative stock may result in a complete wipeout. A small company's attributes can turn negative in one day's notice, without any advance warning or early detection. Purchasing a variety of stocks will not only spread your risk, but will result in you not missing a possible big winner, particularly when this emphasis is speculative. Invest $1,000 in ten different situations (total $10,000) rather than $10,000 in one situation. If one stock appreciates over 1,000 percent that one stock would be worth more than the other nine (your entire portfolio), despite the fact that the other nine stocks may have been market laggers.

Albeit, a small position in a highly speculative situation may also result in an unexpected and explosive accrual of substantial wealth. The concept of emphasizing an accumulation of ten to fifteen speculative and conservative stocks lessens your risk and enhances your total profit potential.

3. Do not buy on margin. All securities involve risk. During the two severe economic recessions of 1974 and 1982, stocks plummeted. Even some of the most prestigious and highest rated A securities had temporary devastating plunges. For example, Sears Roebuck fell from $61 to $15, Con Edison fell from $18 to $3, and GM, Ford and Citicorp A rated bonds fell from $1,000 to $490, et cetera. If a stock drops 50 percent, given time it may come back and may even trade over your original cost.

There are appropriate times when additional purchases are warranted at lower quotes (averaging down). If you purchase 100 shares of stock at $10 a share ($1,000), and it falls to $5 a share, an additional purchase of 100 shares will now cost you $500. Total cost of 200 shares, $1,500. If the stock then rebounds to $7.50 a share (200 shares times $7.50 equals $1,500), you are now even. If it trades back to $10 a share, your original purchase price

(200 shares times $10 equals $2,000), you would now have a net profit of $500 or a 33 percent gain. If on margin (credit), a 50 percent drop in a stock may result in a 100 percent loss—a complete wipeout.

Chances are you may be forced to sell when instead you should have been a buyer at lower levels. In addition, if you are on margin and unexpectedly the company goes bust, you will find yourself in a position of owing your broker additional monies which may be unavailable, thus causing you to dip into savings or sell a potentially favorable security to cover your loss.

The best buying opportunities usually prevail when a company reports lower earnings, and when adverse economic news is widespread. Purchase of stocks immediately after glowing earning reports or after optimistic press releases often result in buying at the top. The best time to purchase is when A) others are advocating the sale of the security, B) you anticipate adverse news (poor earnings performance), C) stock is below book value, and D) the stock is out of favor. Diversity of risk is extremely important.

4. If any stock doubles in value, sell half. You now have a no-risk situation.

5. Have patience. We cannot emphasize the importance of patience, especially in consideration of your goal of long-term capital appreciation. The stock which you are purchasing reflects the inherent potential (good or bad) six months to one year out. Therefore, don't expect the stock to go up the day after you purchase it. Your goal should always be long-term capital appreciation.

When you buy quality, sometimes the gain comes quicker. Milton Bradley (September 1983) at $21 a share was selling below book value. The company was taken over in June 1984, nine months later, at $50 a share resulting in a 138 percent gain, excluding dividends.

STOP-LOSS ORDER

A stop-loss order is an order given to a broker to sell a certain stock when a specified price is reached.

Stop-loss orders are used to:

1. Limit the downside risk after purchasing a stock.
2. Lock in a profit or gain on a stock that was purchased at a lower price.

For example, a stop-loss is placed on National Corporation at $24.50 (now trading at $29 a share). Having purchased this stock two years past at $14.50 and lower, you would have profits at this level. If National Corporation stock is falling, your broker would have instructions to sell at $24.50, thereby protecting or locking in a large portion of your gain.

If you purchased National Corporation at $29 a share, the stop-loss would be insurance against taking a large loss.

As a stock advances, the price of the stop-loss order may be changed (usually higher) to try to maximize the gain.

Stop-loss orders cannot be used for all stocks. Thinly traded and speculative issues may vary 20–30 percent in a week's time. If stopped out (sold out), two weeks later the stock may be trading at substantially higher quotes. Also, a stop-loss order given to a broker at $24.50 automatically becomes a sell-at-market order when the stock reaches the stop-loss price.

For example, Price Computer was selling at $40 a share. You instructed your broker to place a stop-loss order at $32 a share, that is to sell the stock if it dropped to $32 a share. When Price Computer plunged from $33 to $22 in one day's time, chances are you were sold out at $22 a share and not at $32 a share, your stop-loss order. Why? Because your stop-loss order automatically became a market order when the stock traded at $32 a share.

You cannot have thousands of subscribers looking to be stopped out at the same price in the same day, especially in a stock that has poor liquidity (few shares and low volume). To use stop-loss orders across the board on every security would have the effect of causing unnecessarily large widespread losses.

Investors who follow the price of their portfolio daily may not wish to enter a stop-loss order with their brokerage firm. An investor may enter the sell order when the stock trades at his designated stop price. This technique is known as a mental stop-loss order.

In conclusion, a stop-loss order should be used to lock in your profit after a stock advances. A stop-loss order should also be placed at 15% below your purchase price to limit your loss. Chapter 5 will elaborate, specifically referencing stop-loss strategy.

Note: The examples above were factual occurrences, the real names of the stocks being changed.

Chapter V

AVOIDANCE OF DISASTER

Knowing the difference between junk and factual information. Protect your profits. Significance of Standard & Poor's (S&P) stock ratings.

There are many tempting traps that the unwary investor may perceive as a good deal.

Story Stocks: These beguiling inside stories tend to encourage an imaginative buyer to ignore reality, overbuy, and then suffer financial loss when the story turns into a fairytale. To avoid such psychological mistakes, be skeptical of phony financial experts who give you the story and not the figures. Instead, follow financial strategy that has repeatedly produced good results.

Broker's Tips: Brokers are order takers, not financial analysts. For example, a brokerage sales office may be directed to sell a particular stock (work the stock); the sales manager may offer the broker 70 percent of the gross commission instead of the usual 30–40 percent cut. Despite this incentive, the broker may be unaware that his firm is stuck with unwanted stock.

Regardless of this possibility, an informed broker is one who will always tell you of a sudden price change in one of your situations; he will also inform you of news referencing your situation. But if he does give you a tip, let him know from day one that you expect a tip to be accompanied by the company's 10K, 10Q, and Annual Report.

Protect Your Profits: After purchasing a stock, if you have a profit, do not sell it until it drops 15 percent from its high. Many stocks you purchase will ultimately trade much higher than their worth. Stocks going up tend to feed on themselves. If you purchased Ford Motor in 1982 at $11 a share, it did not trade 15 percent below its high until it reached $47 a share in early 1984. Given a book value of $35 a share, at $47 a share the stock was trading $12 ahead of itself. Your stop-loss order at $47 a share would have been placed at $40 a share (15 percent of $47 equals $7). Forty-seven dollars minus $7 equals $40. Always sell half when a stock doubles from your purchase price. Use the 15 percent rule on the remainder of your holdings.

Do Not Buy Up. This rule is in direct conflict with Wall Street thinking. If you take a position (buy a stock) at $20 a share and the stock goes to $30 a share, do not buy more. If you purchased more at $30 a share and the stock dropped to $24 a share you are now a loser, instead of still being profitable to the extent of 20 percent. Wall Street says sell your losers and keep your winners. Follow this rule and you will always lose. You will be selling stocks which indeed should probably be purchased. If you have an undervalued situation, and due to poor market or economic conditions the stock drops, purchase more at the lower quotes (average down). When a stock trades heavy volume after a sizeable upward move and the price does not increase, this is usually a warning the stock is at or near its high (topping out). When a stock trades very little after a substantial decline and does not fall in price, this is usually a sign the selling is just about over. The stock may sit at low quotes for many months (washed out), but generally everyone who wanted to sell at the lower quote has sold and any optimistic news can cause the stock to appreciate substantially. Do not buy stocks immediately after optimistic news is released. Wait a week for the news to get old, then buy the stock.

When placing an order to buy or sell a stock, always first ask the broker the bid and ask quote of the security. All stocks have a bid and ask price. Then inform the broker whether you are buying or selling. Do not quibble for an eighth or a quarter point. If a buyer, pay the price. If a seller, take the bid.

The Newspapers: They will print the news, but it is up to you to interpret it. Throughout the 1980s, many respectable stock market columns were subjected to companies being mentioned by the papers' editors who were paid by the companies to mention this situation. The editors and other insiders purchased the stocks at lower prices before the favorable mention and profited when the general public purchased the same stocks at higher prices.

Unfortunately, anyone who purchased these stocks was ignorant about fundamental analyses. As delineated in chapter 2, not one stock mentioned was selling less than twice its book value. Most were selling at astronomical P/E ratios, and many of the companies mentioned had weak current ratios. The public was buying paper, not value.

The Securities and Exchange Commission (SEC) brought this scam into the limelight. Those responsible may receive harsh treatment, but those uninformed who lost monies will not recoup their losses. As an investor you will be subjected to many articles. Brokerage firms and public relations firms will fill your mailbox with brilliant multicolored brochures. Investigate before you invest. It is an impossible task for newspaper editors and the media to investigate all situations on which they must report daily. It is important you realize that when you are touted, most of the stocks mentioned to you were previously purchased by those touting you. You are probably price they paid for a security. Chances are, you may receive a quarterly report from a mutual fund stating they own 100,000 shares of Con Edison and Milton Bradley at their recent highs. The quarterly report would not reveal that they sold MCI at $7.50 a share, down from $28, or that they sold Coleco at $10 a share, down from $65 a share.

If you choose to purchase a stock because it is low, wait until after the end of the quarter. Chances are, it will be trading lower. Of course, there is no guarantee the stock won't trade even lower in the upcoming quarter. If you are going to bottom-fish, be patient. Albeit, if you want to sell a stock that is trading near its high, chances are it will be higher just before the quarter ends.

In conclusion, when making an investment decision, fundamental analysis is the No. 1 criteria: Current Ratio, P/E Ratio, Book Value, Long Term Debt, et cetera. Window-dressing by the institutions may result in additional gains or fewer losses for the individual investor. Coleco at $30, down from $65, was purchased by thousands of investors. Yet, if they waited for the institutional managers to cover-up, they could have bought it at $10. Avon at $37 was thought a good buy at $27. Two weeks before the end of the 4th quarter, 1984, it was at $21. As an individual investor you only have to answer to yourself. Use the institutional politics to your advantage.

Earnings and Dividend Rankings for Common Stocks

The investment process involves assessment of various factors—such as products and industry position, corporate resources and financial policy—with results that make some common stocks more highly esteemed than others. In this assessment, *Standard & Poor's* believes that earnings and dividend performance is the end result of the interplay of these factors and that, over the long run, the last to hear the good news. And you may be buying at the top when those informed are selling.

INTERPRETING STANDARD & POOR'S (S&P) STOCK RATINGS

The managers of the billions of dollars of institutional monies pay close attention to the S&P ratings, which range from A+, the highest, to C, the lowest rating. Most institutions follow guidelines when investing monies.

If a stock is rated B−, chances are, only $100 million in total available funds is allowed to be invested in B− situations. A rating increase to B will entail a possible $1 billion of invested funds applied to the B category stocks. A B+ rating will entail $50 billion, an A− rating will mean a $100 billion, and an A or A+ rating, $300 billion.

In other words, if a fund manager invests $10 million in a B− stock and it collapses, he may very well risk his job. If the $10 million was invested in a B+ or higher rated stock, and it collapsed, his investment was justified.

Increases in S&P ratings ultimately result in higher quotes due to additional monies available for investment in these stocks. Decreases in S&P ratings usually result in lower stock quotes.

Window-dressing: The institutional funds represent approximately 75 percent of all monies in the market. The managers of these hundreds of billions of dollars must answer to their shareholders and superiors. All of the mutual and pension funds are required to issue quarterly reports to their respective shareholders.

Near the end of the quarter, stocks which were down or close to their yearly lows are usually sold by the institutions, thus causing even lower stock quotes, and stocks near their highs are purchased, thus enforcing higher quotes.

The institutions do not have to reveal the per share

the record of this performance has a considerable bearing on relative quality. The rankings, however, do not pretend to reflect all of the factors, tangible or intangible, that bear on stock quality.

Relative quality of bonds or other debt, that is, degrees of protection for principal and interest, called creditworthiness, cannot be applied to common stocks, and therefore rankings are not to be confused with bond quality ratings which are arrived at by a necessarily different approach.

Growth and stability of earnings and dividends are deemed key elements in establishing *Standard & Poor's* earnings and dividend rankings for common stocks, which are designed to capsulize the nature of this record in a single symbol. It should be noted, however, that the process also takes into consideration certain adjustments and modifications deemed desirable in establishing such rankings.

The point of departure in arriving at these rankings is a computerized scoring system based on per-share earnings and dividend records of the most recent ten years—a period deemed long enough to measure significant time segments of secular growth—to capture indications of basic change in trends as they develop, and to encompass the full peak-to-peak range of the business cycle. Basic scores are computed for earnings and dividends, then adjusted as indicated by a set of predetermined modifiers for growth, stability within long-term trend, and cyclicality. Adjusted scores for earnings and dividends are then combined to yield a final score.

Further, the ranking system makes allowance for the fact that, in general, corporate size imparts certain recognized advantages from an investment standpoint. Conversely, minimum size limits (in terms of corporate sales volume) are set for the various rankings, but the system provides for making exceptions where the score reflects an outstanding earnings-dividend record.

The final score for each stock is measured against a scoring matrix determined by analysis of the scores of a large and representative sample of stocks. The range of scores in the array of this sample has been aligned with the following ladder of rankings:

A+	Highest	B+	Average	C	Lowest
A	High	B	Below Average	D	In Reorganization
A−	Above Average	B−	Lower		

NR signifies no ranking because of insufficient data or because the stock is not amenable to the ranking process.

The positions as determined above may be modified in some instances by special considerations, such as natural disasters, massive strikes, and nonrecurring accounting adjustments.

A ranking is not a forecast of future market price performance, but is basically an appraisal of past performance of earnings and dividends, and relative current standing. These rankings must not be used as market recommendations; a high-score stock may at times be so overpriced as to justify its sale, while a low-score stock may be attractively priced for purchase. Rankings based upon earnings and dividend records are no substitute for complete analysis. They cannot take into account potential effects of management changes, internal company policies not yet fully reflected in the earnings and dividend record, public relations standing, recent competitive shifts, and a host of other factors that may be relevant to investment status and decision.*

*Source: *Standard & Poor's*

Chapter VI

THE UNITED STATES GOVERNMENT

Our country's policies, politics and laws, continually being changed can make or break the market and your choice of investments.

Our government's economic policy and spending preference should be considered when investing. If vast amounts of the United States' financial resources are being poured into aero-space, defense, and electronic-related technology, then you can feel comfortable in investing in these areas. Solar energy projects and telecommunications also hold promise of steady growth throughout this decade.

Remember that the government has the power to raise or lower margin requirements (a vital factor in stock market movement).

Margin: The amount borrowed by the customer from his broker to buy a security is called margin. Currently a customer may purchase $4,000 worth of stock by putting up $2,000, using $2,000 of the brokerage firm's money. Under Federal Reserve regulations, the initial margin required since 1945 has ranged from the current 50 percent of the purchase price up to 100 percent. During the late

1920s it was reputed that customers put up only 10% of the purchase price. This resulted in one of the greatest boom and bust periods in the history of the financial markets.

Equally important, the government can increase or decrease interest rates and regulate taxes. All of these measures can drastically affect the investment situation. For example, with recent new tax legislation enforced by the Internal Revenue Service, many oil and gas tax shelters went out of existence. When a tax was invoked on gasoline with proceeds directed to rebuilding roads and bridges, billions of dollars in revenues were created for cement companies. Deregulation imposed on the airlines was great for the consumer but bad for most airline stocks.

Another potent government influence is the Individual Retirement Account (IRA) which supports prices of stocks rated B+ or higher, yielding current income. High interest rates set by the Federal Reserve might enhance the mobile home industry, but damage the conventional home business. Even the home-state roots of the president can be a very important consideration for the investor: under President Johnson, the Texas oil industry boomed, and under President Reagan, California's aerospace and defense industry grew considerably.

Awareness of government influences can increase or decrease your financial status, but the prime consideration is always your thorough evaluation of the fundamental position of a company. You don't purchase a stock selling for 10¢ a share, given 100 million shares outstanding, just because it's in aerospace or the government-favored areas; on the other hand, backed by the fundamentals of sound financial statements, speculating can be very rewarding.

TAX REVISION

Capital Gains and Losses

Major Changes

- Maximum tax rate on long-term capital gains incresed from 20 to 28 percent.

- Maximum tax rate on short-term capital gains reduced from 50 to 38.5 percent in 1987 and 28 percent in 1988 and future years.

- Maximum tax rate on regulated futures contracts will remain close to 32 percent in 1987 and will be reduced to 28 percent in 1988.

- All net capital losses will offset ordinary income dollar-for-dollar up to $3,000 per year.

- Installment sale treatment is repealed for sales of publicly traded property entered into after December 31, 1986.

Interest Expense

Major Changes

- Mortgage interest deductions permitted only on a primary and one secondary residence.

- Mortgage interest deductions allowed on loans only up to purchase price of property plus improvements, unless the loan proceeds are used for educational or medical expenses.

- Investment interest deductions limited to net investment income.

- Deductions for consumer interest will be eliminated subject to transitional rules.

- Interest on debt incurred to fund an IRA will no longer be deductible.

Retirement Planning

Individual Retirement Accounts

- $2,000 IRA deduction ($2,250 for spousal IRAs) retained for all employees not covered by another retirement plan.

- $2,000 IRA deduction for employees covered by another retirement plan retained if adjusted gross income is less than $40,000 ($25,000 on single returns).

- IRA deductions phased out for individuals with adjusted gross income between $40,000 and $50,000 ($25,000 and $35,000 on single returns).

- Non-deductible contributions allowed for employees not entitled to deduct IRA contributions.

- Earnings on nondeductible contributions not subject to income tax until withdrawn.

- Interest on debt incurred to fund an IRA will not be deductible.

Tax Investments

Major Changes

- Deductions for losses from tax investments limited to income from tax investments.

- Losses from working interests in oil and gas ventures remain fully deductible.

- Losses from real estate rental activities allowed to offset up to $25,000 of other income subject to phase-out as adjusted gross income exceeds $100,000.

- Investment tax credits repealed for property placed in service after December 31, 1985.

- Depreciation schedules revised for property placed in service after December 31, 1986, generally requiring machinery, equipment and real property to be written off over longer periods of time.

- Rehabilitation tax credits reduced to 20% for certified historic structures and to 10% for buildings placed in service before 1936.

Business Taxation

Major Changes

- Effective July 1, 1987, corporate income tax rates reduced from a maximum tax rate of 46 to 34 percent.

- Effective January 1, 1987, corporate capital gains alternative tax rate increased from 28 to 34 percent.

- Owners of unincorporated businesses, including partnerships and sole proprietors, as well as S corporations, may benefit from the lowering of individual tax rates.

- Dividends-received deduction reduced from 85 to 80 percent.

- Investment tax credits repealed for property placed in service after December 31, 1985. The amount of unused investment tax credits that are carried forward from prior years will be reduced by 17½ in 1987 and 35 percent in 1988.

- Depreciation schedules revised for property placed in service after December 31, 1986, generally requiring machinery, equipment and real estate to be written off over longer periods of time.

- Maximum annual elective deferral by an eligible employee is limited to $7,000 in 401(k) plans.

- Employees elective deferrals of up to 7,000 annually to certain Simplified Employee Pension (SEP) plans will be permitted.

- Key employees will no longer be permitted to deduct interest on loans from any qualified retirement plan.

- Business meals and entertainment deductions limited to 80 percent of expense.

- Alternative minimum tax preferences expanded to include one-half of "untaxed reported profits" and tax-exempt interest on private purpose bonds issued after August 7, 1986.

- Research and development tax credit reduced to 20 percent and extended through 1989.

- Interest deductions on business-owned life insurance restricted to interest on loans of $50,000 per employee.

- Tax deferral on earnings from annuity contracts held by corporations and other entities described as non-natural persons is eliminated.

Corporate Tax Rates

Income Bracket	Pay Base Tax of	Plus This Percentage of Amount over Lower Bracket
1986		
$ 0	$ 0	15%
25,000	3,750	18%
50,000	8,250	30%
75,000	15,750	40%
100,000	25,750	46%
1,000,000	439,750	46% plus 5% on excess over $1,000,000 or $20,250, whichever is less

1987
New rates effective July 1, 1987

1988		
$ 0	$ 0	15%
50,000	7,500	25%
75,000	13,750	34%
100,000	22,250	39%*
335,000	113,900	34%

*Benefit of lower bracket taxation is phased out for income over $100,000

Tax reform should extend the recent flow of investment funds to financial assets as disinflation expectations become more widespread. The many incentives for reevaluation of corporate and individual portfolios imply that a more volatile financial market environment lies immediately ahead.

Although marginal tax rates will be lowered to levels not seen in the post-World War II era, effective rates for many individuals may well rise. Because of the increased after tax cost of using credit, prices for many tangible assets will continue to adjust accordingly. Most important, the consumption spending made possible by credit subsidies will become less appealing as consumers' nonmortgage interest deductions are pared back. That, we believe, has negative implications for nominal domestic economic growth at a time when worldwide growth is slow. As those perceptions become more widespread, interest rates should continue to move irregularly lower.

One of the more notable changes in the investment equation is the increase in the effective tax rate on capital gains. Eliminating the capital gains deduction implies and equal footing for stocks and bonds because capital gains, interest income, and dividends would be taxed at equivalent rates. As a result, we expect the yield differential between stocks and bonds to narrow over time. Bonds and bondlike stocks should become even more attractive portfolio components in the future.

Chapter VII

OPTIONS

A cautious approach. Making a killing with a smidgen of your funds. The "Three time" rule.

A call option is the right to purchase 100 shares of a given stock for a specified price within a given period of time.

A put option is the right to sell 100 shares of a given stock for a specified price within a given period of time. The purchaser of a put expects the price of the stock to go down.

Puts and calls expire within 9 months. Both are traded in the market and approximately 350 put and call options are listed daily in local financial newspapers.

A right is a call with an expiration date, usually less than one year and in most cases, usually less than three months.

A warrant is a call with an expiration date usually exceeding one year. Buying puts and calls involves the highest degree of risk and rewards in the financial markets. You buy a call to make a 1,000 percent gain and a put to make a minimum 200 percent gain. It is estimated over 80 percent of all option buyers are wiped out. So when you buy a call you go for it all (Sell half if you double your money and let the rest ride).

SUGGESTIONS FOR INCREASING YOUR ODDS

When you buy a call, always buy the call that gives you the longest time frame, usually the nine-month call. Be prepared to buy the call three successive times. In other words, if you purchased a nine-month call and lost monies, buy the call again for the next nine months and then again for a third time. You are now in a position to own the call for not only nine months out, but for twenty-seven months or over two years. Most purchasers of calls lose money not because they didn't pick the right stock, but because they picked the right stock at the wrong time.

For example, in November 1982 the call option for Con Edison, the right to buy the stock at $20 a share up until August 1983, was selling for $25 ¼. For $25 you had the right to buy 100 shares of Con Edison stock at $20 per share, for $250 you had the right to buy 1,000 shares of Con Edison (ten calls) at $20 per share. In August 1983 Con Edison traded at $25. From $25 (¼) the option rose to $500 ($5). An initial gamble of $250 would consequently be worth $5,000.

Options require patience, endurance, and the will to stay. The best time to begin your three time option program is when a stock looks sick, which is usually when it's at its lowest price. If you had purchased the Con Edison option in 1981 or early 1982 you would have lost money. The third time around you would have made a killing, but you would have lost $500 before hitting it right.

Always play options with no more than 5 percent of your funds. Buying CDs or Treasury Notes which offer consistent income, then purchasing options with all or half the interest income is a sensible approach. Given this scenario you will never lose your principal, and if you lose on that option (and many times you will incur a 100 percent loss), it will be a tax-deductible item.

To reiterate: Know your risk–reward ratio and avoid the overplay, a frequent mistake of the uninformed investor. Then you can have fun with options—being always aware that you will lose some and win some.

LEVERAGE

Leverage is defined as increased power or advantage. Most investors do not have the funds to purchase many of Wall Street's blue chip stocks or to purchase the quantity of shares to have any meaningful effect on their financial position. If, for example, you figured that Exxon, Ford Motor Company, Santa Fe Southern Pacific, and Xerox were undervalued, purchase of 100 shares each of these four stocks would require an investment of $18,000.

Purchase of Stock				Purchase of One Nine Month Call		
100 Shares of Exxon	@ $53	= $5,300		$55 Call @ $1½		= $150
100 Shares of Ford	@ $47	= $4,700		$50 Call @ $1½		= $150
100 Shares of Santa Fe	@ $33	= $3,300		$35 Call @ $2¼		= $225
100 Shares of Xerox	@ $47	= $4,700		$50 Call @ $1		= $100
		$18,000				$625

The above calls are termed *out of the money* calls because all of the stocks are trading below the strike price (exercise price) of the call. As such, the total cost of $625 represents time premiums, or the right to buy the underlying stocks within nine months. If none of the stocks trade above the strike price, you will lose your entire investment. But if only one stock appreciates 20–30 percent and the other stocks trade below the strike price, you will still come out ahead.

For instance, if Ford Motor were to appreciate 24% (say from $47 a share to $58 a share) the call would trade at $8. You have the right (option) to purchase Ford at $50 a share despite Ford's market value of $58 a share. If you sold the call you would receive $800. It must be noted that in 1983 most of these stocks appreciated 50–100 percent. A $625 speculative purchase if held for nine months, the duration of the call, would have brought you over $15,000. It's a game the small investor should always be aware of. And you do not have to go to Las Vegas or Atlantic City to participate, for this type of gambling is legal in all fifty states.

You can purchase in-the-money calls, which are options (contracts) trading above the strike price. The cost of in-the-money calls reflect a smaller premium because the call has intrinsic value and leverage less than out-of-the-money calls. The Ford Motor call (mentioned below) gives you the right to purchase Ford common stock at $45 a share. Since Ford is trading at $47 a share the call is worth a minimum of $2. You are paying $4.50 for the call or a $2.50 point (dollar) premium. In our first example, you are paying $1.50 for a Ford Motor call exercisable at $50 a share. Since Ford Motor is trading at $47 a share, it would have to appreciate three points (to $50 a share) to be in-the-money, plus another one and a half points for you to be even since your cost is one and a half or $150 per call. Your premium would be three points plus one and a half points or a total of four and a half points, $450. Still, your total cost is one and a half points, or $150. When you purchase an out-of-the money call, your entire cost is a premium, and theoretically your investment is a negative investment. If at the expiration date Ford Motor does not appreciate more than $3 a share, you will lose your entire investment.

Purchase of One Nine Month In-the-Money Call			Market Price of Stock
One $50 Exxon	Call @ $4½	= $450	$53
One $45 Ford	Call @ $4½	= $450	$47
One $30 Santa Fe	Call @ $5	= $500	$33
One $45 Xerox	Call @ $4	= $400	$47
		$1,800	

We prefer out-of-the-money calls. With a mere $625 (3.5 percent of $18,000) you have $18,000 of leverage. The latter example would require $1,800 or 10% of your funds and subject you to possible greater losses.

If you were to invest the $18,000 in government securities or Certificates of Deposit yielding 7 percent or more ($1,260), your cash position would still increase even if you had a total loss regarding your call option position ($1,260 interest income less $625, the cost of your calls). More importantly, you have not risked any portion of your $18,000 principal.

Sooner or later the call options will reward your patience in using the three time rule.

In our examples we have used call (buy) options or contracts. The same strategy applies to put (sell) options. Albeit, 90 percent of investors purchase stocks for appreciation and only 10 percent (the speculators) take short positions or purchase puts. Your broker will assist you in obtaining up-to-the-minute quotes on all put and call contracts.

Barron's lists all put and call quotes in alphabetical order. Most financial newspapers list daily quotes. Put and call contracts are listed on the Chicago Board Options

Exchange, the American Stock Exchange, the Philadelphia Stock Exchange, and the Pacific Stock Exchange. Do not be alarmed if your put or call is not printed from time to time. If no trading (buys or sells) occurred that particular day, the newspapers will not print the quote. All options have a bid and an ask price, and your broker has immediate access concerning this information.

A new breed of options is gaining investor enthusiasm: The *S&P 500 Index, The Value Line Index, The New York Stock Exchange Composite,* et cetera. These options are based on the broad movements of hundreds of stocks.

You will have much greater success in buying calls on a few undervalued situations which you have scrutinized. These indexes are usually sought by professionals to hedge against their current stock holdings; professionals who do not trust their own judgement.

Chapter VIII

INSIDER TRADING — INSIDER INFORMATION

10K's and 10Q's. Patience.

The law states that no one should purchase or sell a company's stock while possessing material information not yet made public. In reality, most investors can obtain material public information, usually from the company's 10K and 10Q reports. The Securities and Exchange Commission (SEC) sells a monthly publication, costing approximately $90 a year, that lists purchases and sales by company officers and directors. This is a must reading for investors, because if a stock you hold is being sold by insiders (company officers and directors), the stock should not be in your portfolio.

Consider the logic of the following example. When Ford Motor was $25 a share in 1982, five to ten insiders sold the stock. Ford has over 100 insiders, though, and those who sold had cause for regrets when, eighteen months later, Ford traded at over $60 a share. On the other hand, if the president and chairman sold substantial holdings, you should also be selling. The SEC publication lists the quantity of sales and purchases, the price of the stock, when stock was sold or purchased, and the total amount of stock still held by the seller or purchaser. The list is usually two months old, which is an advantage, not a disadvantage. If an insider holds 500,000 shares and sells 50,000 shares, it is not significant; but if he sells 200,000 shares or more, it is a portentous signal. No one, especially someone in the know, sells a large block of his stock unless it is going to be worth less in due time.

Insider purchasing is one of the tools for successful investing. If insiders purchase stock prior to good news, it is illegal; but the SEC will overlook such purchases if made prior to six months before the optimistic news was released. The authorities figure that the stock in six months could trade lower, and in that time frame anything (negative) can occur. Fact is, many of the large multibillion dollar companies plan ahead and have forecasts and budgets prepared monthly, budgeting twenty years out. Getty Oil was taken over at $128 a share in 1984; but two years prior to the announcement, tens of millions of shares were purchased by Middle Eastern interests at $41-$64 a share. When you come across heavy insider buying, chances are good news is forthcoming, but not immediately. Insiders, usually company executives, purchase the stock six months or more before the happy event in order to be legal buyers.

The Williams Act of 1934 requires anyone with an ownership of 5 percent or more of a class of stock to file a 13D schedule. It would be rare that you, as an individual, would know if someone is purchasing large blocks of stock before Wall Street knows, and by the time Wall Street lets it be known, the stock will have already made its move.

If you followed our principles outlined in the previous chapters, chances are your selection of a stock would be correct and those limited insiders who are selling would be wrong.

Conclusion:

Don't be concerned by insider sales unless the chairman or president of the company liquidates a substantial position of his holdings. Heavy accumulation by insiders is an indication better times are ahead. Also don't be in a hurry to buy when Wall Street advertises insiders are buying the stock. That's when the stock is trading higher due to the news. Wait a few weeks. In most cases, the stock will fall back (trade lower) when the news is old and all but forgotten.

Chapter IX

INTEREST RATES

The most accurate stock market indicator.

The most important rate that influences stock prices is the federal funds rate, the rate that leads all other money rates. It is the rate one commercial bank charges another commercial bank to borrow monies (loans) that are in excess of $1 million. All other interest rates (called money rates) that are used by Wall Street and bankers are strongly influenced by the federal funds rate, including those that dealers pay to finance their security (stock and bond) holdings. Analysts also watch the federal funds rate for clues to Federal Reserve credit policy.

For example, if Chase Manhattan needs monies, it borrows from Citibank or Bank of America. During 1986, the rate fluctuated between 5½–8 percent. If it costs the bank 6 percent to borrow, the bank will lend to customers at 10–18 percent. The higher the federal funds rate, the more it costs companies to borrow, thus discouraging investment while increasing interest costs of companies. When company costs increase, profits decrease: when profits decrease, stocks go down.

Note also the importance of the United States government. Through its bank, the Federal Reserve, the government controls interest rates. The Federal Reserve, the bank's bank, can make interest rates rise or fall by controlling the money supply.

KNOW THESE INTEREST RATE TERMS

Prime rate: The rate commercial banks charge their customers. In reality, no customer borrows at the prime rate. The customers, GM, IBM, et cetera borrow at ½–1 percent above the prime rate. Smaller companies usually borrow at 2–3 percent above the prime rate. A small company that pays these high rates is jeopardizing its financial health, especially if inflation is at a low rate. During disinflation, it is vital that you invest in companies with little or no debt.

Discount rate: the rate the U.S. government's bank, the Federal Reserve, charges other banks. The banks borrow from the government at a lower rate, for example 5½ percent (the discount rate), and charge customers the prime rate, 7½ percent. The banks cannot borrow all of their needed monies from the government at 5½ percent due to reserve restrictions. That's where the federal funds rate, the interest rate charged by one bank to another, comes in.

Call money: the rate charged to brokerage firms based on stock exchange collateral. The brokerage firms usually charge their customers 1–2 percent above the call money rate when a customer buys stock on margin. The brokerage firms' largest source of income is not commission charged to customers, it's the profit (interest) made from customers who are buying stocks on margin. All brokers are influenced to open margin accounts for all of their clients. You now know why.

Certificates of Deposit (CDs): rates paid to individuals or others when the bank borrows monies. Usually CDs or loans to the bank are in denominations of $10,000 or more.

The banks advertise and compete to borrow these monies from individuals. The more they borrow, the more they can loan out at the prime rate plus, or to their credit card users who pay 18% plus.

Treasury Bills: when the U.S. government borrows, it issues Treasury Bills, usually in $10,000 denominations. T-Bills usually have a time span (maturity) of three months to six months. Treasury Bonds and Notes have maturities ranging from one to thirty years. Treasury Bills, Notes, and Bonds are the safest investments because the principal is guaranteed at maturity by the United States government.

Conclusion:

Changes in the federal funds rate usually preceed changes in the prime and discount rates. An unexpected move in the prime or discount rate will cause a major stock market reaction. If the federal funds rate is moving up, it is a sign the Federal Reserve is tightening the money supply and the prime and discount rates will be increased, resulting in a lower stock market. If the federal funds rate is decreasing, the Federal Reserve is loosening the money supply and the prime and discount rates will be decreased, resulting in higher stock quotes. Interest rate movements are the most accurate stock market indicator.

Chapter X

CONCLUSION

The best Wall Street has to offer.

EMOTIONS

The psychological attitude of millions of investors is the most important (short-term) influence on stock prices. When investors are pessimistic, stocks sell off (go down) and when investors are optimistic, stocks trade up.

In times of highly optimistic and pessimistic stock market environments, emotional investors incur additional losses and unemotional investors profit more so. Emotional buying and selling of stocks result in most investors ignoring a company's fundamentals.

It is not unusual to purchase a stock based on solid fundamentals and be subjected to a temporary decrease in the stock's prices because of mass psychological investor pessimism. Albeit, fundamental analyses always prevail and as such, all of your investment decisions must be unemotional. Easier said than done. In essence, if you cannot invest strictly on the fundamentals of a company and ignore the emotional market trends, don't invest. Your shrewdest buys will be in times of depressed market conditions (when others are selling) and your largest profits will be when others are highly optimistic, ignoring company fundamentals and purchasing stocks at prices far in excess of the company's per share evaluation. No one, not even the most experienced analyst or technician nor any publication will be able to consistently pinpoint the exact high or low price of a company's shares or the short-term stock market's trend, for no one can predict the behavior patterns of mass investor psychology. Despite the fact you may have purchased the right stock at the wrong time, patience will reward your fundamental evaluation.

Our publication was written to condense the important aspects of your investment decisions.

Thousands of other pages have been written to guide you, the investor. We believe we have presented the most important aspects of financial awareness. Other factors that are imperative in regard to your financial decisions include total return, yield to maturity, cash flow, the big eight, the specialists and/or market makers.

TOTAL RETURN

Total return is important when considering conservative stocks. Total return is price appreciation plus dividend or interest income. Dividend income is obtained from stock payouts, usually quarterly. Interest income is obtained from bond payouts, usually semiannually. For example:

	Price When Purchased	Price When Sold	Percentage Gain	Total Return
Con Edison	5/76 @ $8½	8/84 $27½	+224%	+358%

In this example, Con Edison appreciated 224 percent in price, excluding dividend income. Reflecting the thirty-one quarterly dividend payments (while the stock was under recommendation), holders of the stock received approximately $10.54 in dividends during the recommended time span. The dividend income ($10.54) plus the price appreciation ($19.00) equals the total return.

Utility stocks and high yielding industrial stocks that have secure financial balance sheets are attractive situations for conservative investors, especially in view of the fact that these companies consistently raise their annual dividends. Dividend increases ultimately result in higher stock quotes.

YIELD TO MATURITY—BONDS

Use the following as an example. The current yield on the Ford Motor bond maturing in 1999 was 8.7 percent when it was originally issued at (par) $1,000 per bond. The bond in July 1982 was trading at $520 and new bondholders (those who purchased the bond at current quotes) would still receive $87.00 per year in interest income. The current yield being 16.4 percent at a purchase price of $520 per bond.

The bond will mature in 1999 and bondholders will receive the par (redemption) value which is $1,000 per bond. But built into the purchase is a hidden yield. Besides receiving the current yield (16.4 percent) bondholders purchasing at $520 per bond would receive $480 more when the bond matures. From 1982 through 1999, bondholders would receive an additional $17 per year or a total of $480 over their purchase price. The $17 per year translated into yield would add an additional 3.3 percent a year if the bond was held to maturity.

The yield to maturity is the current yield of 16.4 percent plus the hidden yield of 3.3 or 19.7 percent.

Deep discount bonds—bonds purchased well below their par value—are especially recommended for conservative investors and for Individual Retirement Accounts (IRAs), provided the bond is of a financially secure company.

Note: Both examples were recommended to subscribers of the F.X.C. Investors Corporation Research Service.

CASH FLOW

Cash flow is an accounting term that is becoming extremely popular on Wall Street. Cash flow is the amount of cash that actually flows into a corporation. It is net income plus depreciation and amortization. Depreciation and amortization are expenses deducted from income which do not result in an outflow of cash.

Southern Company — Year Ended Dec. 31, 1986

Revenues	$6,123,985,000
Expenses	4,974,912,000
Depreciation & Amortization	429,404,000 (Book entry)
Net Income	$ 719,669,000
Net Income Per Share	$3.00
Net Income:	$ 719,669,000
Add: Depre. and Amort.	429,404,000 (Book entry)
Cash Flow:	$1,149,073,000
Cash Flow Per Share	$4.79

The above example reflects $3 a share in earnings, but actually Southern Company made $4.79 a share in cash. The company's earnings are much stronger than reported and the cash flow per share ($4.79) far exceeded Southern Company's annual dividend in 1986 of $2.04 per share. In October 1985, Southern Company raised the dividend to $2.04 annually, $.51 a share quarterly.

More important, there are times when a huge loss is reported by a company but given the depreciation and amortization book entry, the cash flow is positive.

> Note: F.X.C. initially recommended Southern Company to its subscribers August 1982 at $12.50 a share. The stock then yielded over 13 percent and was trading at 75 percent of its book value of $16.78.

PAN AM CORPORATION

Year Ended Dec. 31,

	1984	1983
Net loss:	($206,836,000)	($51,025,000)
Add: Depreciation and amortization:	207,679,000	215,823,000
Cash flow:	$843,000	$164,798,000

Pan Am made headlines, reporting a huge 1984 loss. Yet the corporation received more cash than it spent in 1984.

Cash flow is an indication of a company's financial strength and earnings potential, more so than the company's earnings, and is also a reflection of a company's dividend and interest paying ability. Cash flow also includes other noncash adjustments, but depreciation and amortization account for the bulk of noncash expenditures.

A corporation with more cash than it needs for day-to-day operations may pay off debt, buy back its own shares on the open market or raise its dividends.

Cash flow should also be considered when purchasing shares of a company but only after careful consideration is given to earnings prospects, financial strength and the anticipated strength of the company's industry. You do not want to buy an oil company's stock when the price of oil is declining and the industry's trend is down.

> Note: Despite Pan Am's positive cash flow, in October 1985 Pan

Am was selling for $8½ a share, thirty-four times its book value of $.25 a share. Everyone on Wall Street buying the stock due to takeover rumors, most ignoring the fundamentals.

THE BIG EIGHT

The big eight is a term that's used regarding the eight largest accounting firms. These accounting firms audit 90 percent of the companies listed on the New York Stock Exchange (NYSE). Their clients account for 94 percent of all sales in the U.S. and 90 percent of income taxes. The big eight in order of size are:

1) Peat Marwick Main
2) Arthur Andersen
3) Coopers & Lybrand
4) Price Waterhouse
5) Ernst & Whinney
6) Arthur Young & Company
7) Touche Ross
8) Deloitte Haskins & Sells

Invest conservative monies in companies which are audited only by one of the big eight.

FINANCIAL STATEMENTS

There are more than 20,000 public corporations trading on the various stock exchanges and in the Over-The-Counter markets. *Moody's Manual* contains information on over 17,000 companies. Another cause of investors losing monies is financial statements that are not prepared in accordance with federal regulations (Section 13 or 15d of the Securities Act of 1934).

If the figures are not correct, your investment in the stock is subject to substantial or complete loss. We suggest subscribers confine investments in companies audited by one of the big eight.

There is no assurance your investment will increase because of competent auditors. But if the company's accountant is one of the big eight, in most cases, your investment decision will be based on an accurate financial presentation in the company's Annual Report, Quarterly (10Q) and Annual (10K) reports, filed as required with the federal and state regulatory agencies. Today, there are many companies reporting manipulated figures and when the government eventually intervenes, it is too late for the investor to recoup his losses.

THE SPECIALIST

The specialist is your biggest competitor. Approximately 400 individuals, members of the New York Stock Exchange, buy your stock when you sell and sell your stock when you buy. Your broker gives your order (his customer's order) to one of the specialists who is assigned that particular security. Hence, there is always a buyer when you decide to sell your stock and a seller when you decide to buy. The specialist's function is to maintain an orderly market in the securities registered to him and to record limit orders in his book.

All stocks have a bid and ask price. When asking your broker for a quote always ask for the bid and ask price, not the last or closing price.

For example, you instruct your broker to buy 100 shares of Ford Motor. The last quote may be $41.50 a share. Your broker tells you it is $41.50 a share. Yet the stock may be bid $41. Ask $41.25. If you give your broker a market order, his brokerage firm may buy the stock at $41.25 and charge you $41.50. When asking for a quote, first get the bid and ask, then instruct your broker if you are buying or selling. A broker once told me he had a client who always gave him an order to purchase stock 50¢ below the market price. When asked for a quote he always told this client the stock was 75¢ higher than the ask price. The broker always made the sale.

The specialist always has a direct line to inside information and in most cases, big money is made by these elite 400. When a company reports earnings, the specialist gets the information before the general public.

IBM won a major lawsuit, and prior to this information the stock was trading at $300 a share. The specialist had been trading the stock in the $300 area for a few days. When the specialist received the news, he changed IBM's stock price from $300 bid–$301 ask to $320 bid–$321 ask. The specialist opened the stock higher. When the news was released to the public, they purchased frantically at $321 and higher. The specialist made a killing. The reverse could have happened, and the specialist would have lost heavily.

As a matter of fact, at that time, the largest Over-The-Counter brokerage firm shorted IBM stock, believing IBM would lose the decision. This was a costly error in judgement, for that brokerage firm went bankrupt shortly after. In the Over-The-Counter (OTC) market the small Over-The-Counter firms act as specialists and maintain markets in specific OTC listed stocks.

More recently, Avon Products announced it was going to purchase 20 percent of its shares on the market. The specialist opened the stock from $22 to $25.50 a share. The crowd purchased at $25.50 a share. One week later the stock traded back to $23.50 a share.

Conclusion: Do not purchase a security when very good or very bad news is released. Wait a week or two for the emotional buying to end. If bad news is reported, chances are those who purchased on margin will be shocked out of the stock, if not from the bad news, then from their broker. Margin selling tends to feed upon itself and as the stock goes down, more and more selling will prevail. In 1983 Coleco Industries traded from $65 to $16 a share. Apple Computer went from $31 to $14 in 1985 and Storage Technology from $14 to $2. All of the above examples reflected astronomical book values, price earnings ratios and extremely poor financial statements in comparison to their stock market prices. Again, we go back to the roots of disaster—fundamental analyses. Incidentally, the specialist is also an expert in investor psychology.

THE BEST WALL STREET HAS TO OFFER

The Individual Retirement Accounts (IRAs): Approximately $40 billion will be invested annually in IRAs and Keoghs (self-employed retirement plans). Twenty to thirty billion dollars will be invested in the stock and bond market. These huge figures represent a continuous flow of demand for high yielding conservative securities.

Throughout this decade the huge amount of monies invested annually will alter the market's course. Most of these monies will seek total return: conservative high yielding securities. In ten to fifteen years, IRAs may account for 25 percent of the stock and bond market's total evaluation. The dividends and interest also being continually reinvested. These monies will probably not be withdrawn for 20 years or more for they represent tax free retirement monies invested for the long term by individuals. Another consideration is when the forty-and-over group reach retirement age, the children of today will commence their retirement investing. Every year millions more will enter the work force, adding additional funds to IRAs, presenting a continual flow of buying demand. Securities (with no or low yield) other than takeover candidates may underperform the market for years to come.

It is important that you, the investor, confine most of your conservative funds to cash yielding securities.

EPILOGUE

Creating an awareness of indirection was my objective in bringing forth this publication. A guide informing the mis-informed and to assist you in recognizing Wall Street's street-walkers, those who will sell you anything to obtain your monies; street-cleaners, those who will try to take all your monies; and street-wise, those who will use sophisticated techniques to seduce your monies.

If I have helped to preserve a significant portion of your hard-earned monies and indeed increase your overall financial status, I will have attained my goal.

The script of my success rests upon your achievements.

GLOSSARY OF ACRONYMS

AICPA	American Institute of Certified Public Accountants
Amex	American Stock Exchange
BSE	Boston Stock Exchange
CBOE	Chicago Board Options Exchange
CBT	Commodity Board of Trade
CEA	Commodity Exchange Act
CFTC	Commodity Futures Trading Commission
CRD	Central Registration Depository
EDGAR	Electronic Data Gathering Analysis and Retrieval
EFTS	Electronic Funds Transfer System
FASB	Financial Accounting Standards Board
FCPA	Foreign Corrupt Practices Act
FOIA	Freedom of Information Act
FRR	Financial Reporting Release
GAAP	Generally Accepted Accounting Principles
GSA	General Services Administration
ITS	Intermarket Trading System
ITSA	Insider Trading Sanctions Act
MOSS	Market Oversight and Surveillance System
MSE	Midwest Stock Exchange
MSRB	Municipal Securities Rulemaking Board
NASAA	North American Securities Administrators Association
NASD	National Association of Securities Dealers

NASDAQ	National Association of Securities Dealers Automated Quotation System
NMS	National Market System
NSCC	National Securities Clearing Corporation
NYSE	New York Stock Exchange
OCC	Options Clearing Corporation
OECD	Organization for Economic Co-operation and Development
OMB	Office of Management and Budget
OTC	Over-The-Counter
Phlx	Philadelphia Stock Exchange
PIC	Productivity Improvement by Computer
POB	Public Oversight Board
PSE	Pacific Stock Exchange
RFA	Regulatory Flexibility Act
SAB	Staff Accounting Bulletin
S&L	Savings and Loan Association
SECO	SEC-Only Registration Program
SECPS	SEC Practice Section
SIC	Special Investigations Committee
SIPC	Securities Investor Protection Corporation
SRO	Self-Regulatory Organization
ULOE	Uniform Limited Offering Exemption